# John Logie BAIRD

## Dr Mike Goldsmith

HODDER
Wayland

an imprint of Hodder Children's Books

© 2002 White-Thomson Publishing Ltd

Produced for Hodder Wayland by
White-Thomson Publishing Ltd
2/3 St Andrew's Place
Lewes
BN7 1UP

*Editor:* Anna Lee
*Designer:* Derek Lee
*Picture Researcher:* Shelley Noronha, Glass Onion Pictures
*Science Panel Illustrator:* Derek Lee
*Map Illustrator:* Tim Mayer
*Consultant:* Dr Brian Bowers, Senior Research Fellow at
   the Science Museum, London
*Proofreader:* Philippa Smith

Cover and title page: John Logie Baird with some of his early
television equipment.

Published in Great Britain in 2002 by Hodder Wayland, an imprint
of Hodder Children's Books.

**British Library Cataloguing in Publication Data**
Goldsmith, Mike, Dr.
John Logie Baird. – (Scientists Who Made History)
1. Baird, John Logie 2. Inventors – Scotland – Biography –
juvenile literature
I. Title II. Lee, Anna
621.3'88'0092

ISBN 0 7502 3943 3

Printed in Hong Kong

Hodder Children's Books
A division of Hodder Headline Limited
338 Euston Road, London NW1 3BH

*Picture Acknowledgements:* Camera Press 18; Corbis 21, 27; Hodder
Wayland Picture Library 11, 26, 45; Hulton Archive *cover, title page,*
22, 23b, 24, 25, 37; Mary Evans Picture Library 36; Peter Newark's
Pictures 35; Popperfoto 16, 38, 39l, 41b, 42; Science and Society
Picture Library 4, 5, 7, 31, 32, 39r; Science Photo Library 12;
Scotland in Focus 6; Scran 8, 9, 10, 13, 14, 17, 19, 20, 23t, 28, 29,
33t, 33b, 40, 41t, 44.

# Contents

# Seeing by Electricity

WILLIAM TAYNTON FIDGETED nervously, wondering what he was about to see. A few minutes earlier he'd been working away at his desk in the solicitor's office where he was an office boy. Suddenly the scruffy man who worked upstairs had burst in, muttered something about an experiment and ushered him into his laboratory. Now William sat in front of a strange piece of machinery made of bulbs, wires, wheels and motors.

The laboratory was almost in darkness, but William could hear the man talking to himself and flicking switches. Then the machinery began to hum with power, discs started to turn and suddenly a dazzling beam of light started to flash repeatedly into William's eyes. Only the thought of the money the man had thrust into his hand kept him sitting there. Across the room, the screen in front of the man

BELOW: *The apparatus Baird gave to the Science Museum, London, which he used in some of his earliest successful television experiments.*

showed nothing but a dim blur. Patiently, he adjusted the controls and the blur grew sharper. Then a face appeared on the screen. Dim, flickering, but unmistakable – it was the face of William Taynton.

The man gave a cry of delight and rushed downstairs to tell people about the miracle he'd achieved. It was October 1925 and John Logie Baird had televised a human being for the first time.

LEFT: *One of Baird's first television pictures of a human face.*

# Before TV

JOHN LOGIE BAIRD was born in 1888 in Helensburgh, a small town near Glasgow, Scotland. In those days there were no radios, no cars and no planes. Although electric lighting and telephones had both been invented, they were still rare in private homes. Most people worked long hours and, when they had time for entertainment, they usually read books or visited the theatre.

### Early experiments

Long before Baird's experiments with television began, scientists had experimented with the idea of transmitting moving images. In 1884 Paul Nipkow had applied for a patent on the type of scanning disc that would be an important part of Baird's system. Nipkow's disc allowed the image of an object to be converted to a ray of light of changing brightness, or for the ray to be converted back to the image of the object. However, the bulbs and motors needed to turn it into a working television had not yet been invented.

**IN THEIR OWN WORDS**

*'Like so many inventions, television was developed by many inventors over many years rather than springing ready-made from one single act of genius.'*

IAN SINCLAIR IN HIS BOOK ABOUT THE INVENTION OF TELEVISION *BIRTH OF THE BOX*, 1995.

BELOW: *Baird's birthplace, Helensburgh, on the River Clyde in Scotland.*

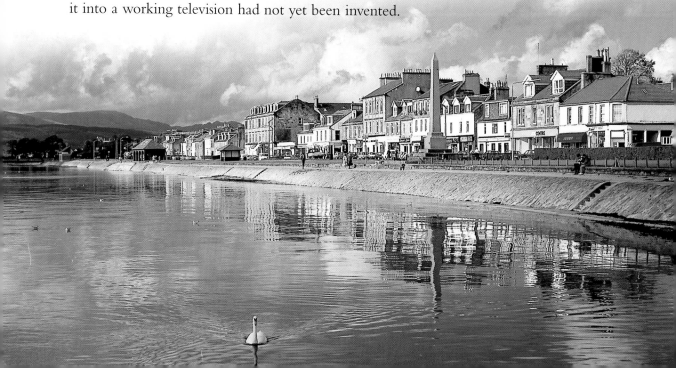

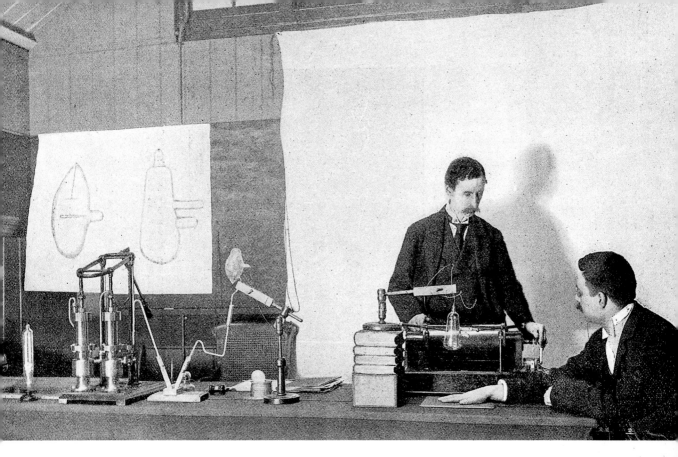

Baird's first televisions were mechanical (see panel). They used moving parts, and Baird stuck to this approach for many years. An alternative idea was suggested in 1908 by Alan Campbell Swinton, a Scottish electrical engineer: television could be entirely electronic and contain no moving parts at all. But Campbell Swinton himself doubted that his own solution would work. However, by the 1920s, scientists such as Philo Farnsworth and Vladimir Zworykin were experimenting with the idea of electronic television. They worked in the United States, but the battle between their systems and Baird's would be fought in Britain (see pages 36–7).

ABOVE: *Alan Archibald Campbell Swinton (left) demonstrating the power of X-rays to the Royal Photographic Society. The seated man's hand is resting on a photographic plate and the bulb above it is generating X-rays that will produce an image of the bones of the hand.*

## MECHANICAL AND ELECTRONIC TELEVISION

All televisions start by sampling different parts of an object in turn. This process is called scanning. In a mechanical television system (see page 25), a spinning disc converts the image of an object into a light-ray. The light-ray is transformed to an electrical signal by a light-sensitive cell and this signal is changed back to an image at the receiver by means of a lamp and another spinning disc.

In an electronic system (see page 34), light from the object is converted to a pattern of electrical charges by an electronic camera. At the receiver, the signal from the camera is converted to a stream of electrons, which reconstructs the image on a screen. The screen is coated with chemicals so that it glows where the electrons hit it.

# Early Years

JOHN LOGIE BAIRD was the youngest child of a
reasonably well-off family. His father was a Presbyterian
minister and he had two sisters and a brother. He was a
healthy baby until he developed bronchitis at the age of two.
This led to Baird's lifelong ill-health, which became an
important part of the story of television.

## First inventions

Baird was fascinated by technology from an early age, and set
up a successful telephone exchange that he used to keep in
touch with three of his friends. The exchange
came to an abrupt end when a local cab
driver became entangled in the wires and
complained. But Baird didn't waste
the wires: along with a generator,
he used them to convert his gas-
lit house to electric light,
causing a sensation in
Helensburgh. He charged up
the batteries to power the
lights with a dynamo driven
by a water-wheel under the
kitchen sink. (In a dynamo, a
coil of wire is rotated in a
magnetic field, which
generates an electric current
in the wire.)

RIGHT: *Baird in 1890 with his
mother, Jessie, and siblings Jean,
James and Annie. Baird is sitting
on his mother's knee.*

## IN THEIR OWN WORDS

*'I was, I am told, a healthy and energetic infant until, at the age of two, I contracted a very serious illness… I was ill for several months, and remained for a time a delicate weakling. However, I remember little of all this except for a faint image of myself under an apple tree on a red blanket, the first impression to remain on my mind.'*

BAIRD IN *SERMONS, SOAP AND TELEVISION*, 1941.

ABOVE: *Baird as a boy outside his home in Helensburgh.*

Baird's attempt at flying wasn't so successful. He built a huge kite with a friend, who launched him off the roof in it. Baird crashed into his garden and the experience put him off flying for the rest of his life.

As a boy Baird loved reading and his favourite author was H.G. Wells, whose books are full of amazing inventions – including television. Baird's very first experiments with television took place when he was a teenager, but they didn't achieve a great deal. He had heard of a metal called selenium, which reacts to changes in light by changing its resistance to electricity. Baird tried to make a light-sensitive cell from selenium, but ended up with burnt fingers instead.

# DIFFICULT DAYS

Baird quite liked the first school he attended, but was transferred to another, very strict one after only a few months. He once said that his years there were the worst of his life. Things didn't improve much when, aged eleven, he went to Larchfield Private School. Sport was taken very seriously here (two hours a day, followed by a cold shower), but almost no maths was studied and science wasn't taught at all. Baird was often in trouble and did badly in all his lessons, partly because of his frequent illnesses. However, he was fascinated by practical things. He started a camera club and bought a broken-down three-wheeled car that he repaired and then travelled around in, accompanied by clouds of smoke and ear-splitting noises.

BELOW: *The Argyll Street cricket team. Baird is at top left and the future film star, Jack Buchanan, is at bottom right. Buchanan later helped Baird with his work on television.*

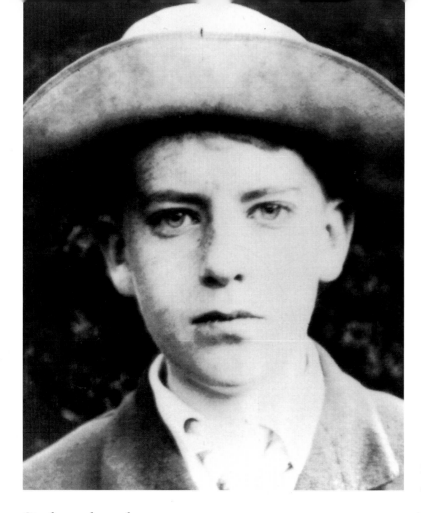

LEFT: *A photo Baird took of himself, aged about twelve.*

## Study and work

In 1906, Baird left Larchfield and went to the Royal Technical College in Glasgow to study electrical engineering. He remained there for eight years – far longer than usual because of his bad health. As part of his studies Baird took several temporary engineering jobs, which he hated. His first job was to carve grooves in pieces of metal so that they could be used as parts of motors. It was a cold, boring, dirty task, and Baird was determined that his future wouldn't be spent doing such uninteresting jobs.

After college Baird went briefly to Glasgow University where he spent one of the happiest periods of his life. He intended to become a Bachelor of Science, but in 1914 the First World War began and, like many other young men, Baird left his studies to join the army. But a brief medical examination was enough to show that he was 'unfit for any service.' So, in 1915, Baird had to find himself a full-time job.

### IN THEIR OWN WORDS

*'I trudged to work in the cold dawn with sordid, miserable and grimy poverty on every side, coughing and choking, either sickening for a cold or trying to recover from one.'*

BAIRD DESCRIBING HOW HIS EARLY JOBS MADE HIM REALIZE HOW DIFFICULT MOST PEOPLE'S LIVES WERE. BAIRD IN *SERMONS, SOAP AND TELEVISION*, 1941.

# The Salesman

AFTER SEVERAL DEPRESSING months, Baird answered a newspaper advertisement and was soon working for the Clyde Valley Electrical Power Company. He called it a 'horrible job', and so it was. One of his tasks was to supervise the repair of faulty cables – sometimes in the middle of the night. He had a phone by his bed and when there was a loss of electrical power – as there frequently was – he'd receive a call telling him to get up immediately.

LEFT: *Baird at the Clyde Valley Electrical Power Company in 1915.*

His job was to supervise the workmen who dug up the road in an attempt to track down the faulty cables. The conditions often brought on terrible colds, and Baird's employers were convinced that it would not be safe to give him a better job, as he might spend too much time off sick.

## Cold feet

Baird knew that his ill-health could prevent him finding and keeping a good job, and realized that the only answer was to make money through his own efforts. He knew television would take time and money to develop, so instead he invented a new type of sock!

Baird was always troubled by cold feet, and as a child he dreamed of a world covered with a thin layer of warm water to paddle in. A more realistic way of keeping his feet warm was to invent a special damp-proof sock to be worn under normal socks. His 'thermostatic undersocks', as he called them, were simply ordinary un-dyed socks sprinkled with a moisture-absorbing powder. This would have melted away the first time they were washed, so the socks weren't really much use. But what Baird lacked in terms of a successful product, he more than made up for with his skill as a salesman.

**IN THEIR OWN WORDS**

*'To break my career seemed to those about me the act of an irresponsible madman, throwing away all my expensive training. But if the choice was between hopeless slavery and madness, I preferred madness.'*

BAIRD IN *SERMONS, SOAP AND TELEVISION*, 1941.

BELOW: *'The Lodge', Baird's family home in Helensburgh, where he spent his weekends while he worked for the power company.*

# SELLING SOCKS

Baird tried all sorts of original ways of selling his socks. He asked his friends to go to shops and demand them, sent a huge model tank covered with advertisements to roam the streets and, most successfully of all, employed women to wear big signs advertising them. In those days it was unheard of for women to do this sort of thing and they – and the socks – became famous. Baird was soon making a lot more money from the socks than from his job at the electricity company, which didn't please his employers. They were even more unimpressed with his next experiment. He decided to use the electrical power available to him to make himself some diamonds!

His plan was to send an enormous electrical current through a thin piece of carbon embedded in concrete. He hoped that the great heat and pressure that would result would turn the carbon into a diamond. What actually

BELOW: *Sandwich-board women advertising Baird's undersocks in Glasgow.*

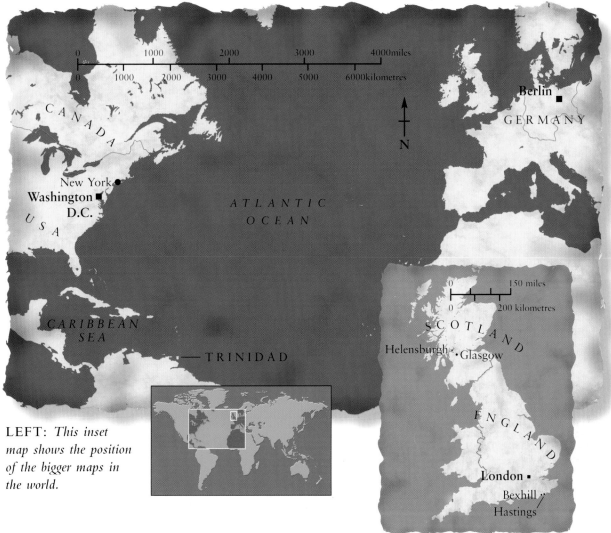

LEFT: *This inset map shows the position of the bigger maps in the world.*

ABOVE: *These maps show the different places Baird lived during his life, and other places mentioned in this book.*

happened when he switched his set-up on was that a large area of Glasgow was plunged into darkness. Though he soon restored the power supply, his employers were horrified, and Baird decided to resign before they could fire him.

Sadly, as usual, Baird's health let him down. A long period of illness left him unable to run his sock company, and he was forced to close it down – although it had made him quite a lot of money. Baird decided to use the money to escape the cold, miserable climate that constantly made him ill. In 1919 he set off for Trinidad, an island in the Caribbean, just off the north coast of South America.

# ESCAPE

Baird was expecting to find a warm tropical paradise where he would at last be free of illness. But as soon as he had forced his way through the crowds and suffocating heat to his hotel room, he collapsed with dysentery.

When he had recovered a little, he moved from the expensive hotel to a boarding house and started his latest money-making project – selling cotton and safety-pins. Unfortunately, hardly anyone wanted to buy them, so Baird tried something different. There were plentiful supplies of mangoes, citrus fruits, guavas and sugar on the island, so he moved to a small village on the edge of the jungle and set

BELOW: *Port of Spain, Trinidad. Baird came here in 1919, hoping to restore his health. Unfortunately, he fell seriously ill with dysentery shortly after his arrival.*

up a jam-making factory. It wasn't a success. As soon as he and his assistants started to heat the mixture of fruit and sugar, swarms of insects arrived. From then on it was a constant battle to protect his sugar supplies and beat off the invasions of ants, flies, spiders and beetles.

Baird finally managed to bottle some of the jam he made, but found it no easier to sell than the safety-pins and cotton – the many insects stuck in it probably didn't help! As had happened over and over again, it was illness that really ended this venture, when Baird was struck down by a mysterious fever.

Baird may have experimented with television in Trinidad too – there are stories of strange flashing lights from his hut, and some say that flickering images were seen there. But whatever the experiments were, Baird never mentioned them himself.

After nine months, Baird made his way back to Britain once more, this time to London.

## IN THEIR OWN WORDS

'The floor of my bedroom swarmed with insects, chiefly enormous cockroaches; great spiders ran up and down the walls, and weird insects whose names I did not know flew in and out in swarms, whilst mosquitoes continually enfolded me in a cloud.'

BAIRD DESCRIBING LIFE IN TRINIDAD IN *SERMONS, SOAP AND TELEVISION*, 1941.

BELOW: *The hut in Trinidad where Baird made jam.*

# BAIRD THE BUSINESSMAN

Back in London, Baird tried a string of different money-making ideas. He sold the jam he'd brought with him to a sausage maker (he said that sausage-makers would use any ingredient that 'wasn't actually poisonous'). He answered dubious newspaper advertisements and lost money on risky ventures. He also took over a shop and sold an odd mixture of goods: honey, because it was cheap, and fertilizer, because it came with the shop. One of his most successful schemes was to buy cheap soap and resell it as 'Baird's Speedy Cleaner'. It did so well that he could afford to employ staff to help him sell it, and for a while business went well.

BELOW: *Baird's Speedy Cleaner had to compete with well-known brands of laundry soap, but Baird's skill as a businessman meant it sold well.*

## Leaving London

During his stay in London, Baird moved many times. For a while he settled in the boarding house of Mr and Mrs Impett. Mr Impett had a job at the Post Office Engineering Department, and Baird constantly questioned him about his work. Eventually Baird's curiosity, combined with his odd behaviour (such as making faces in the mirror at meal times) resulted in him being asked to leave. At about the same time a rival, Oliver Hutchinson, brought out Hutchinson's Rapid Washer Soap, and Baird once more became ill. He sold his company to Hutchinson and, giving up on London for a while, moved to Hastings, on the south coast of England.

In Hastings, Baird's creative mind came up with another string of schemes and inventions. He developed a glass razor that wouldn't rust, but that was also too dangerous to use. His pneumatic (air-filled) shoes were huge boots with half-inflated balloons in them. They were meant to make walking easy, but he had to limp home after they burst on their first trial. So Baird returned to the invention he'd had in mind since he was a teenager: television.

### IN THEIR OWN WORDS

*'Coughing, choking and spluttering, and so thin as to be almost transparent, I arrived at Hastings station, assets totalling approximately £200, prospects nothing.'*

BAIRD DESCRIBING HOW POOR HE WAS ON HIS ARRIVAL IN HASTINGS IN *SERMONS, SOAP AND TELEVISION*, 1941.

BELOW: *Baird with Oliver Hutchinson. Although they were rivals for a while, they later worked together to promote Baird's television.*

# The First TV Show

BAIRD HAD A good idea for the basic design of a
working television system, but almost no money. He had to
build it with whatever bits and pieces he could afford,
including pieces of coffin-wood, a biscuit tin, a hatbox and a
knitting needle.

The final result consisted of a pair of discs that were
turned by an electric motor. A bright beam of light from an
electric lamp shone onto a cardboard cross, casting a black
shadow on the spinning discs. In this first simple television
there was no screen: the viewer looked at the spinning
discs themselves.

BELOW: *Baird working at his home in Hastings.*

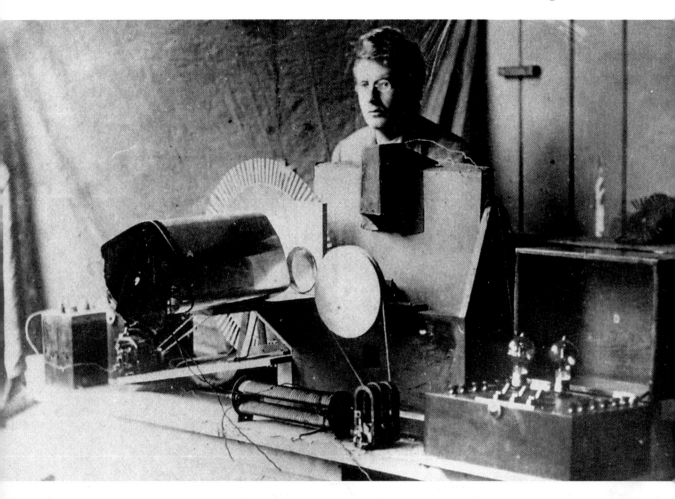

## Early television

Research into television had been underway for many years, with some partially successful systems being built as early as 1909. However, it wasn't until the early 1920s that experimenters all over the world began to develop systems that really worked. The first demonstration of a working television system, in which moving images were transmitted by radio signals, was made by Charles Francis Jenkins, an American inventor, in the USA in December 1923. Others, including Baird, claimed to have developed working systems before then, but Jenkins' demonstration was the first to be seen by reliable witnesses.

In any case, Baird knew that his shadow image, although a great encouragement, was only the start. He was determined to build a television system that people would want to buy, a television that could show not just shadows but pictures with light and shade.

### IN THEIR OWN WORDS

'Sending pictures over distances was possible. He had done it! At that moment he saw into the future. Sooner or later, he told himself, there would be pictures all over Britain – maybe all over the world. Great events would be watched as they took place. The Cup Final, the Derby, Test Matches, royal processions, sessions of Parliament – people would be able to watch these things in their homes.'

JOHN ROWLAND IN *TELEVISION MAN, THE STORY OF JOHN L. BAIRD*, 1966, WRITING ABOUT BAIRD'S FIRST SUCCESSFUL ATTEMPTS TO TRANSMIT A MOVING IMAGE.

(THE CUP FINAL IS A FOOTBALL MATCH AND THE DERBY IS A HORSE-RACE.)

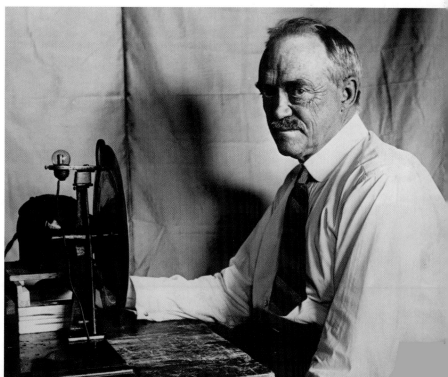

RIGHT: *The American inventor Charles Francis Jenkins, with parts of a television.*

# RISKS AND REWARDS

The construction of his first working television was an enormous step forward for Baird, but he knew that there were still many problems to overcome. As well as the obvious technical difficulties, he also had to cope with finding money for his equipment. At this point he could hardly afford to eat properly and was about to be thrown out of his flat!

Baird's TV experiments were risky. One day he received a massive electric shock, which the local paper reported as a 'loud explosion.' For his landlord, who had always been unhappy about Baird's use of his room as a laboratory, it was the last straw. He asked Baird to leave, so Baird returned to London.

BELOW: *Baird experimenting with one of his many mechanical televisions.*

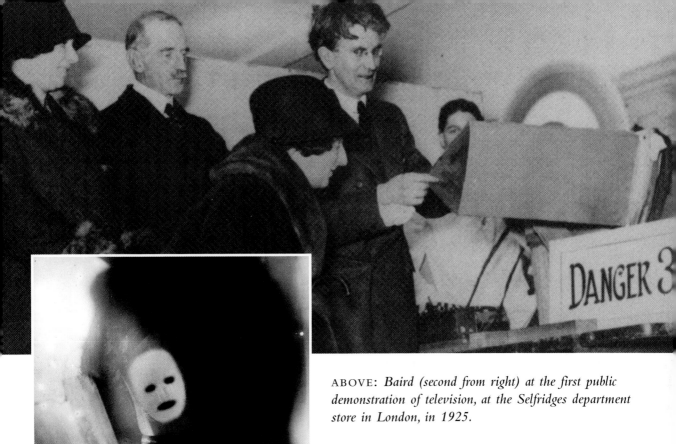

ABOVE: *Baird (second from right) at the first public demonstration of television, at the Selfridges department store in London, in 1925.*

LEFT: *The world's first publicly televised image – a mask televised by Baird at his Selfridges demonstration. At this stage, Baird's system could not show shades of grey.*

## In the public eye

Baird was determined to make television work, but to do that he needed both funding and publicity. After many frustrating meetings in which he and his ideas were rejected as crazy, he finally talked Gordon Selfridge, the owner of Selfridges department store, into paying for a public demonstration of television – the first in the world.

The demonstration ran at Selfridges in Oxford Street, London, from 1 to 22 April 1925. It attracted a lot of interest from scientists, as well as shoppers. They looked down long funnels to see the black silhouettes of masks and other objects. Although it was a stressful experience for Baird, who was constantly on hand to make sure the equipment neither broke down nor electrocuted anyone, the demonstration was a success. Very shakily, television had arrived.

ABOVE: *Baird with part of his 1926 TV transmitter. The bulbs brightly illuminated the subject (either one of the dummies Baird is holding, or a person), which was then scanned through the hole in the centre of the equipment.*

## IN THEIR OWN WORDS

*'One of the visitors who was being transmitted had a long white beard, part of which blew into the wheel [of Baird's experimental television]. Fortunately, he escaped with the loss of a certain amount of hair.'*

BAIRD IN *SERMONS, SOAP AND TELEVISION*, 1941.

# OUT OF THE SHADOWS

Baird knew that the televisions he had built so far were too simple to be anything more than novelties. He still needed a way of transmitting images with light and shade, rather than silhouettes. Helped by his former rival Hutchinson and by other assistants, he struggled to improve his system. He tried huge spinning discs equipped with bulbs and lenses – that sometimes exploded in a hail of glass lumps and cardboard, or bounced around the laboratory, smashing themselves to pieces. But finally, in October 1925, he was ready. He set up a ventriloquist's dummy called Stookie Bill in front of the apparatus and switched it on, and Bill's image appeared on the television screen.

Excitedly, Baird rushed downstairs to the office below his laboratory and grabbed an office boy called William Taynton. William was reluctant but, for a small fee, he sat in position in front of the machine. Baird adjusted his equipment – and an image of William appeared, the first person to be televised.

### Success in view

Now Baird had a working system it was time to attract some serious interest. He invited some members of the Royal Institution and a reporter from *The Times* to a demonstration on 26 January 1926. His visitors were surprised to find that the address was not a laboratory but Baird's tiny flat.

It was so small that the forty of them could not all fit in at once, and they had to take it in turns to watch the demonstration in his room while the rest waited on the stairs. Despite the conditions, the visitors were impressed. Baird's television was beginning to be taken seriously.

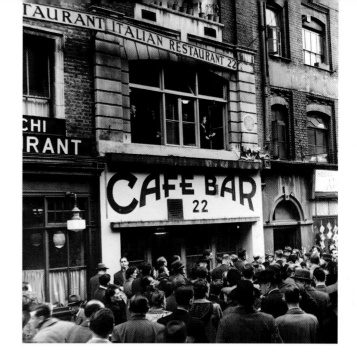

RIGHT: *A plaque to commemorate Baird's achievements being unveiled in 1951 outside 22 Frith Street in London, Soho, where Baird experimented with television in the 1920s.*

## BAIRD'S MECHANICAL TELEVISION

In the earliest of Baird's television systems to show light and shade, a beam of light from a spinning Nipkow disc scanned an object and a light-sensitive cell reacted to the strength of the light reflected from the object. The changing signal from the cell was used to make a lamp brighten and dim, and the light from the lamp shone through the holes in another spinning disc, forming an image of the scanned object on a screen.

This diagram shows the basic principles of the system. Baird kept the details a secret.

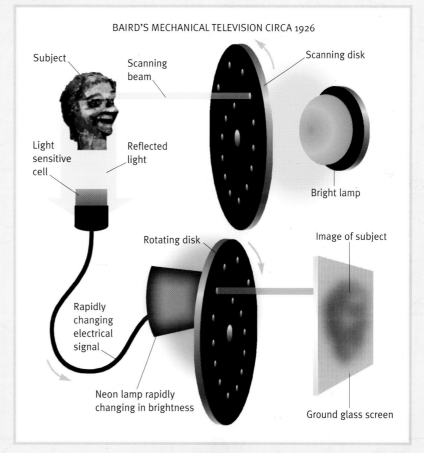

BAIRD'S MECHANICAL TELEVISION CIRCA 1926

Subject

Scanning beam

Scanning disk

Light sensitive cell

Reflected light

Bright lamp

Rotating disk

Image of subject

Rapidly changing electrical signal

Neon lamp rapidly changing in brightness

Ground glass screen

# 'THE TELEVISION MAN'

Baird's demonstration was reported in *The Times* and the *Daily Chronicle*, and he rapidly became famous in Britain as 'The Television Man.' Everyone was excited by the idea that television might be just around the corner and Baird received visits from reporters and scientists. Many were suspicious that television was all a trick.

One problem was that Baird's apparatus needed a great deal of very bright light to work, so he tried to use invisible light instead! His infra-red television was demonstrated to members of the British Association for the Advancement of Science in September 1927, as well as to the Prime Minister, Ramsay MacDonald. They were all amazed that it was possible to see people in total darkness using the system. The same year Baird invented a way of preserving television signals on wax and metal discs to make the first video recordings.

BELOW: *One of the many newspaper and magazine articles about television that followed Baird's demonstration in January 1926. This piece explains the workings of Baird's mechanical television system.*

## Leaving the laboratory

Now that Baird had achieved a reasonably reliable and watchable form of television, he turned to the question of the radio-transmission of television signals. So far his experiments had been confined to laboratories, but now he made contact with Mr H. L. Kirke at the BBC, who agreed to transmit signals for him. Once Baird succeeded in picking up these signals at his

### INFRA-RED

The range of colours from violet through indigo, blue, green, yellow, and orange to red is called the visible spectrum. But beyond it there are invisible rays, including infra-red. We can feel some infra-red rays as heat.

laboratory he knew it was time to take the next step. Along with Hutchinson and some businessmen, he started a company to raise money and to protect his inventions. Baird Television Company Limited was formed on 27 April 1927.

The very next day, Baird and the other members of the company were shocked to see an amazing headline in the paper, reporting a breakthrough in the United States. The headline was 'Television at Last'.

## IN THEIR OWN WORDS

*'I must thank you very warmly for the television instrument you have put into Downing Street... You have put something in my room which will never let me forget how strange is this world – and how unknown.'*

LETTER FROM PRIME MINISTER RAMSAY MACDONALD TO BAIRD, 5 APRIL 1930. BAIRD HAD GIVEN MACDONALD A TELEVISION SET FOLLOWING HIS INTEREST IN THE 1926 DEMONSTRATION.

BELOW: *Dr. Herbert Ives, an American scientist, standing beside the television receiving screen used in the the first inter-city television broadcast, between Washington and New York in the United States.*

# TV in the Air

THE AT&T COMPANY, using nearly a thousand people, had succeeded in transmitting television signals 320 kilometres from Washington to New York. Although he only had eight people to assist him, Baird was determined to do better. So on 24 May 1927 he transmitted a television signal 700 kilometres, from London to Glasgow. Later that year he began to make regular TV broadcasts from a tiny studio in Long Acre, a street in London's West End.

BELOW: *Baird (right) and an assistant on the roof of his Long Acre studio. They are experimenting with Baird's Noctovision system, in which a camera sensitive to infra-red light allowed the viewer to see in the dark.*

RIGHT: *Baird (right) and Sydney Moseley demonstrating three-dimensional television in 1928.*

## Good times

Suddenly, thanks to the company's financiers, Baird and Hutchinson had plenty of money. As well as being an amazing inventor, a skilled promoter and a very determined man, Baird knew how to enjoy himself. He and Hutchinson spent many happy evenings eating and drinking at London's clubs and restaurants. Unfortunately, Baird's delicate health always meant he suffered for days afterwards.

Sydney Moseley, a publicist and financial adviser, joined the company in 1928. Before long he and Baird became good friends. Moseley made sure that there was always plenty of publicity for Baird and his television. Unfortunately, he was often critical of the BBC, which did not help Baird's relationship with the organization.

Baird now had nearly all the ingredients he needed for his television system to succeed – receivers of reasonable quality and reliability, plenty of interest from the public, the media and scientists, enough funding and a basic broadcasting station. But if television was really going to take off, he needed the backing of the BBC. The BBC transmitted radio throughout Britain and beyond, and if Baird could persuade them to transmit television signals too, success would be almost certain. His first discussions with the head of the BBC, John Reith, were quite positive. It seemed all would be well.

### IN THEIR OWN WORDS

'…I met a pale young man named Bartlett who is secretary to the new Baird Television Company. Television! Anxious to see what it is all about … He invited me to go along to Long Acre where the new invention is installed. Now that's something! Television!

'Met John Logie Baird; a charming man – a shy, quietly spoken Scot. He could serve for the schoolboy's picture of a shock-haired, modest, dreamy, absent-minded inventor. Nevertheless shrewd.'

FROM SYDNEY MOSELEY'S DIARY, 1 AUGUST 1928.

# THE THIRD DIMENSION

In 1901, the Italian inventor Guglielmo Marconi had made history when he transmitted the first radio signal across the Atlantic. Now, twenty-seven years later, John Logie Baird was determined to do the same with television. He sent one of his assistants to the United States and, after some failed attempts, succeeded in transmitting the image of several people – including himself – from London to New York in February 1928. Soon after, he transmitted signals to a ship in the middle of the Atlantic Ocean.

## Televisors on sale

No new inventions were needed for these demonstrations, just plenty of power. In fact, one of Baird's purposes was to show that his system was able to work over such huge distances.

## BAIRD'S COLOUR TELEVISION

Between 1928 and 1944, Baird developed five different colour television systems. In the first, the transmitter used three spirals of lenses, one red, one blue and one green, and the receiver used three coloured bulbs. The system gave pictures in realistic colour, though they were less than 3 centimetres square.

Baird's final electronic colour television receiver, which he developed in 1944, used the 'Telechrome' vacuum tube he invented (right). The picture lacked some colours, including green. When he died, Baird was planning a more advanced version with three electron beams that would allow full-colour pictures to be seen.

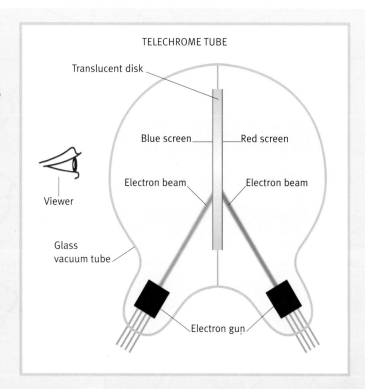

TELECHROME TUBE

Translucent disk
Blue screen — Red screen
Electron beam — Electron beam
Viewer
Glass vacuum tube
Electron gun

But he knew that the low-quality images he could transmit were only the beginning. He dreamed of transmitting a really lifelike image, complete with sound, colour and depth. During the summer of 1928 he developed both three-dimensional and colour television systems, and demonstrated them to scientists and the press on 10 August 1928. At that stage the images were tiny, but it was clear that three-dimensional colour TV was possible. Baird also developed a new type of camera that could be used without artificial light. The next year, his first television sets, called Televisors, went on sale to the public.

On 5 March 1929 there was another demonstration of television. It was intended to convince the BBC that television was now good enough for them to adopt. Among other people, a famous film star called Jack Buchanan appeared. He was a school friend of Baird's who supported him with publicity and money throughout his life. The demonstrations were watched by Members of Parliament, BBC engineers and the Postmaster General, the head of the Post Office, which had the job of issuing broadcasting licences.

BELOW: *A 'Televisor', the mechanical television set Baird developed. The circular section contains the rotating disc, and the tiny viewing screen is on the right.*

BELOW: *Baird and his film star friend Jack Buchanan on the roof of Baird's Long Acre studios, experimenting with a television camera that worked without artificial light.*

### IN THEIR OWN WORDS

*'Baird ... must be credited with having been the first to disembody the human form optically and electrically, flash it piecemeal across the ocean and then reassemble it for American eyes.'*

NEW YORK TIMES, 11 FEBRUARY 1928.

# THE BIG PICTURE

The Postmaster General was impressed, and agreed that Baird could use a BBC transmitter. But Reith, the head of the BBC, didn't like the idea of television, and progress was very slow. However, the German authorities were enthusiastic and Baird began to work with German scientists, transmitting television signals between London and Berlin in May 1929. Perhaps as a result of Baird's work with the Germans, the BBC finally allowed Baird's transmissions from the end of September 1929. At first, the transmissions were silent and were broadcast for only a few hours per week. Then, from March 1930, the BBC allowed the use of a second radio frequency, which meant that sound could be transmitted too.

## Television and cinema

Others were also interested in television, including cinema companies such as the powerful Gaumont-British company. Gaumont-British thought that television would work well in cinemas, showing news programmes. Baird developed better televisions for this purpose. In 1931 he broadcast the Derby, a famous horse race, to an audience at the London Coliseum, using a 1.8 metre by 0.9 metre screen and an improved camera containing a spinning drum of mirrors. The next year he transmitted the Derby again, this time to the Metropole Theatre, London, on a screen three times the size. As a result of demonstrations such as this, Gaumont-British bought into the Baird Television Company.

In September 1931 Baird visited the United States, where it seemed he would be able to sell

BELOW: *Baird's outside broadcast van in use at the 1931 Derby, at Epsom. A large mirror was used to reflect light from the scene to be televised to a spinning drum. The 60-centimetre drum was covered with thirty mirrors, which reflected light to a light-sensitive cell, and the signal from the cell was sent by wire to the aerial of a television transmitter. The broadcast was received up to 200 kilometres away.*

ABOVE: *Baird meets his boyhood hero, H.G. Wells, on board the liner* **Aquitania** *on its way to the United States in 1931.*

his television system. Unfortunately for Baird, the US decided it could not allow a foreign company so much power. But the trip wasn't a complete failure. Earlier that year Baird had met Margaret Albu, a concert pianist, and she joined him in the United States where they were married. They had a daughter, Diana, in September 1932 and a son, Malcolm, in July 1935.

## IN THEIR OWN WORDS

'...a television screen consisting of thousands of little lamps... It was very coarse [basic]... but the effect was brilliant and spectacular... We built a great canvas tent on the flat roof of 133 Long Acre and turned it into a small theatre... A fierce wind was blowing and the tent was none too well fastened down. I was in terror that the whole thing would be blown off the roof, distinguished audience and all.'

BAIRD DESCRIBING THE SHOWING OF THE FIRST TV PLAY IN 1931 IN *SERMONS, SOAP AND TELEVISION*, 1941.

LEFT: *Baird and his wife Margaret soon after their marriage in 1931.*

## CINEMA

In the type of film projector used in cinemas, a broad beam of light passes through a moving strip of film on which photographic images are printed. The beam is then focused onto a screen, where the rapidly changing images can be seen. This is a different process from that used in television, where narrow rays of light or streams of electrons track rapidly across the screen to produce images.

Television receivers, unlike cinema film projectors, can show live action and images from far away. They also allow the same programmes to be seen by millions of people at the same time.

# Winners and Losers

BY NOW BAIRD had convinced people that television was a real possibility. But his wasn't the only system available and the BBC opened its own TV station in May 1932 to trial a different one. Meanwhile, Baird, who realized his TV images were still poor, teamed up with an American inventor called Philo Farnsworth, who visited him in London. Farnsworth had been working on all-electronic television, and Baird developed a new system that used Farnsworth's electronic TV camera, the Image Dissector. In an Image Dissector, a lens projects the scene to be televised onto a piece of metal, which becomes strongly charged with electricity where the image is brightest. The pattern of charge is then converted to an electrical signal that can be converted back to the image again at the TV receiver.

## ELECTRONIC TELEVISION

In an electronic television camera a lens focuses the image onto a light-sensitive plate, creating a pattern of electric charges. This pattern is scanned by an electron beam to produce a signal that is transmitted by an aerial or by cable to the receiver. In the receiver another electron beam reproduces the pattern on a fluorescent screen, which glows brightest where the signal is strongest. For colour television three electron beams are used and the screen has tiny spots of three different phosphors.

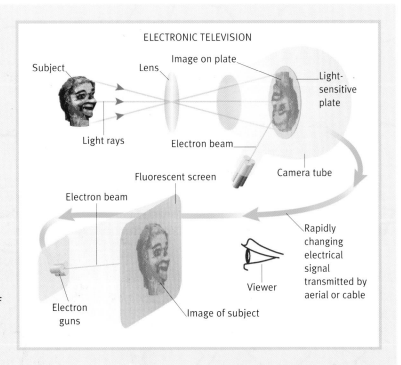

ELECTRONIC TELEVISION

Subject · Lens · Image on plate · Light-sensitive plate · Light rays · Electron beam · Camera tube · Fluorescent screen · Electron beam · Rapidly changing electrical signal transmitted by aerial or cable · Viewer · Electron guns · Image of subject

Baird was also urging the government to invest in an improved 'high-definition' transmission system. This system would deliver much sharper images, but would require expensive new aerials to be built. It would also only work over quite short distances. Baird transmitted his own television programmes using his new system, televising all sorts of things from boxing matches to sea lions.

## A competition is announced

In May 1934 the Post Office set up the Selsdon Committee to decide the future of television. In 1935 the Committee published its conclusion. The good news for Baird was that it agreed that high-definition television was worth funding, but the bad news was that Baird's system would not necessarily be the one the BBC would use. The committee was also impressed by an all-electronic system developed by the Marconi-EMI company (Guglielmo Marconi himself wasn't involved in this work). Rather than choosing between the two systems, the committee announced that there would be a competition between them. Alexandra Palace, London, was selected as the location of the studios and transmitters. Meanwhile, Baird was using part of the Crystal Palace as a laboratory.

The battle for the future of television was about to begin.

RIGHT: *For many years after the trials of the EMI and Baird systems, the BBC's television studios remained at Alexandra Palace. This poster marked the second anniversary of the trials.*

### IN THEIR OWN WORDS

'The committee were finally unable to choose between our apparatus and the apparatus of Marconi-EMI. There was, I think at the time, very little to choose between us.'

BAIRD IN *SERMONS, SOAP AND TELEVISION*, 1941.

ABOVE: *Dancers perform for Marconi-EMI cameras at Alexandra Palace.*

# THE CONTEST

After some initial trials, the contest between the two television systems began on 2 November 1936. Baird won the toss of a coin and his system was used first. The first broadcast included speeches and interviews with Jim Mollison, a famous airman, and with Algernon Blackwood, a popular ghost-story writer. There was also a film – about television. From then on each company transmitted its signals on alternate weeks, for two hours a day except Sundays. Plays, ballets and opera were transmitted, as well as interviews and talks.

Both systems had their problems. Baird's cameras were heavy and clumsy, while EMI's, though lighter, needed more light to work. The EMI system, though it could produce more detailed images with less flicker, could not transmit pre-recorded films as well as Baird's could, nor was it as good at close-ups. Both companies had difficulty persuading actors to appear on television, partly because they were paid less than when they worked on radio. There were only a few thousand televisions on which to watch the broadcasts – they cost about £100, which was as much as a small car! Most televisions were probably watched by many people, as their proud owners invited friends to witness the wonderful new invention they'd paid so much for.

## Sabotage?

On the 30 November there was a disaster: fire broke out in the Crystal Palace, destroying much of Baird's equipment and records.

In February 1937 the Television Advisory Committee made its decision and announced the result of the contest. Baird had lost.

**IN THEIR OWN WORDS**

'The telephone rang and a wildly excited voice informed me that the Crystal Palace was on fire!... I at once rushed out, hatless and in slippers... I managed to elbow my way through to the front of the Palace, which by this time was a seething mass of flames – a wonderful spectacle.'

BAIRD IN *SERMONS, SOAP AND TELEVISION*, 1941.

BELOW: *The Crystal Palace fire, which destroyed many of Baird's records and much of his equipment.*

# THE WAR MYSTERY

Though bitterly disappointed, Baird did not give up his work. Baird Television Company Limited was almost completely taken over by the Gaumont-British company and concentrated on the use of television in cinemas and on selling television sets. The company did well until the Second World War began in September 1939. The government feared that bombers would use the signals from television transmitters as homing beacons, so after a final Mickey Mouse cartoon, television was switched off for the duration of the war.

BELOW: *Film actors at Pinewood Studios being televised by the BBC using Marconi-EMI cameras in September 1937. This was the first television transmission from a film studio. The film was a musical called* **Sailing Along**.

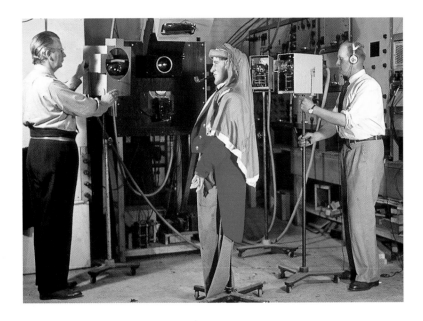

ABOVE: *In 1943, Baird (far left) prepares for the resumption of television transmissions. By now, he was working on electronic television systems.*

ABOVE: *A Baird television set. Though still mechanical, a spinning drum of mirrors was used in place of his earlier spinning discs, to give brighter and sharper pictures.*

## Secret science

As a result, Baird's company collapsed in August 1940 and, with London under threat from bombing raids, Baird moved Margaret and their children to Bude in Cornwall. He stayed on in London, working on an advanced electronic television system. There is evidence that he did much more than this, assisting the armed forces with the development of systems such as night-vision (in which invisible infra-red rays took the place of light), radar (in which radio waves were bounced off objects to detect them) and high-speed signalling. There is also evidence of a secret return to Trinidad, probably related to this war work.

On many nights of the war bombs fell near Baird's house, and it gradually collapsed until he could no longer live in it. He began to sleep in an hotel, returning to work at his house during the day. His health crumbled too, and he had to go into a nursing home in the middle of the war, where he had a heart attack. Despite all this, Baird continued his work.

### IN THEIR OWN WORDS

*'...the continual air raids, which had blown out the windows of my house and brought down all the ceilings, were very upsetting'.*

BAIRD IN *SERMONS, SOAP AND TELEVISION*, 1941.

# THE FINAL BROADCAST

With his usual determination, Baird completed his all-electronic colour television system. It would have been an impressive achievement in a laboratory, but in a half-destroyed house it was amazing. He demonstrated it to the press in August 1944, but it passed almost unnoticed against the background of war.

BELOW: *Baird's home in Bexhill, Sussex, where he and his family moved after the war.*

The war came to an end in May 1945. Soon after, Baird moved back to the south coast with his family, to Bexhill-on-Sea. In February 1946 he suffered a stroke, followed by pneumonia. He became sensitive to cold, and Margaret kept the house as warm as she could. She also found fresh fruit for him, although it was very scarce so soon after the war.

Baird died on 14 June 1946, only a few days after the ban on TV was lifted. But before he died he gave a demonstration of one of his advanced television systems. On 8 June there was a victory parade including marches and speeches. It was televised by both the BBC and Baird, who conducted the operation from his sickbed.

Baird left his money to Margaret, and his friend Jack Buchanan made sure that the Baird Company paid her a pension. It amounted to very little.

Television had many inventors all over the world and there are plenty of arguments about who did what first. As most of the inventors were not in touch with each other, this hardly matters: their work was equally original. But John Logie Baird was certainly a key figure in television history, both in developing working TV systems and, even more importantly, in convincing the press, the government and the public that television was more than a dream.

ABOVE: *Baird with his son, Malcolm, in about 1942.*

BELOW: *Part of the Victory Parade in London, which was televised by both the BBC and by Baird in June 1946.*

---

**IN THEIR OWN WORDS**

*'...a man of genius and destiny who helped shape not only his own age but the decades to come.'*

FROM THE BOOK *VISION WARRIOR, THE HIDDEN ACHIEVEMENT OF JOHN LOGIE BAIRD* BY TOM MCARTHUR AND PETER WADDELL, 1990.

# The Legacy of Baird

AFTER BAIRD'S DEATH, any remaining interest in him and his television faded. The rival systems took over completely and were adopted by countries all over the world. However, although all modern television systems are entirely electronic, the mechanical scanning system that Baird used is still used in photocopiers, weather satellites and most computer scanners.

In the United States in 1951, colour television was introduced, and inventions like infra-red remote-control, video-recording and stereo sound followed. More recently, the introduction of digital technology has brought television to an incredible level of sharpness and clarity. In a digital system, signals are represented by strings of coded numbers.

Live broadcasts are made from all over the world, and from beyond: from the moon's surface and from probes

BELOW: *In 1948, televisions were still expensive and few families could afford them.*

hundreds of thousands of kilometres out in space. There are closed-circuit TV systems watching us for a great deal of our lives, and tiny television cameras can be placed inside us to diagnose illnesses. From a few dozen sets in 1929, there are now over a thousand million in operation the world over. They are becoming more reliable and cheaper each year. It's hard to imagine life without them.

Anyone watching one of Baird's television broadcasts would have been astounded at the difference from today's – anyone but Baird. He would probably have been disappointed that they weren't three-dimensional.

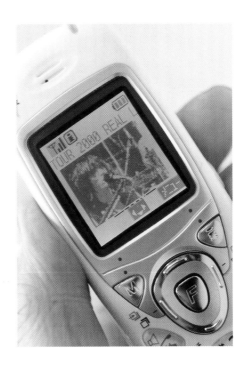

RIGHT: *Baird would have been delighted and astonished to learn how the transmission of images has developed since his death. Today, live events can be watched on a mobile phone. This picture shows a Japanese rock group performing live.*

## TELEVISION TODAY

In a modern television, signals from television transmitters, satellites, cable companies or video recorders are picked up by an aerial or conducted by a cable. Inside the television set, the signals are decoded and amplified. The sound signal is sent to a loudspeaker and the picture signals go to three electron 'guns'. These guns send out streams of tiny electrical particles called electrons, as shown in the diagram.

Electromagnets are used to focus these streams on to the television screen and to move them rapidly across it. The screen is coated with chemicals called phosphors that glow in red, blue or green when the electron streams hit them. The patches of glowing colour are so small and close that they merge into an image. As the picture signal changes, the images move.

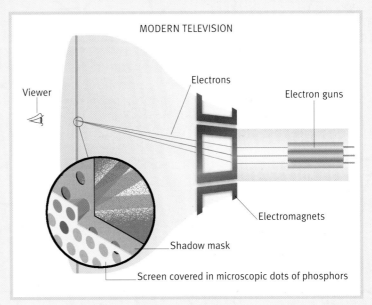

MODERN TELEVISION

Viewer

Electrons

Electron guns

Electromagnets

Shadow mask

Screen covered in microscopic dots of phosphors

# Timeline

### 1884

JANUARY: Paul Nipkow applies for patent on the type of scanning disc used by Baird in his early systems.

### 1888

AUGUST: John Logie Baird born in Helensburgh, Scotland.

### 1897

Karl Ferdinand Braun invents the cathode ray tube, which will eventually be the basis of today's television sets.

### 1901

DECEMBER: Guglielmo Marconi transmits a radio signal across the Atlantic Ocean.

### 1906

Lee de Forest invents the triode valve, based on the diode valve invented by John Fleming two years earlier. These valves meant that electrical signals could be amplified, which made radio and television possible.
Baird attends the Royal Technical College in Glasgow where he studies electrical engineering. Baird attends Glasgow University.

### 1908

JUNE: Alan Archibald Campbell Swinton proposes an electronic form of television, the direct ancestor of today's systems.

### 1909

First partially successful experiments with television devices, in Germany, Belgium and France.

### 1911

Boris Rosing builds a primitive television system, which, it is believed, successfully transmits bands of light.
NOVEMBER: Campbell Swinton describes a detailed idea of an electronic television system.

### 1915

Baird begins work at the Clyde Valley Electrical Power Company.

### 1919

Baird goes to Trinidad.

### 1920

Baird moves to Hastings, on the south coast of England, where he experiments with television.

### 1923

DECEMBER: The first definite television transmission, by Charles Francis Jenkins in the USA.

### 1924 or 1925

Valdimir Kosma Zworykin demonstrates a primitive electronic TV system, but the demonstration is only partly successful.

### 1925

APRIL: First public demonstration of television, by Baird.
OCTOBER: Baird succeeds in televising a human being.

### 1926

JANUARY: Baird gives the first public demonstration of a television system that shows light and shade.

### 1927

APRIL: Baird and Oliver Hutchinson form the Baird Television Company Limited. The AT&T Company send television signals 320 kilometres, from Washington to New York.
MAY: Baird transmits television signals 700 kilometres, from London to Glasgow.
SEPTEMBER: Baird demonstrates Noctovision, an infra-red form of television which can be used to see in the dark.

## 1928

JANUARY: Baird transmits a television signal across the Atlantic Ocean.
MAY: Bell Laboratories demonstrates the first outdoor television system.
JULY: Baird demonstrates colour television.
AUGUST: Baird demonstrates a three-dimensional television system.
Philo Farnsworth demonstrates a working electronic camera, the Image Dissector.
SEPTEMBER: General Electric broadcasts the first television drama, *The Queen's Messenger*.

## 1929

MAY: Baird transmits television signals between London and Berlin.
JULY: Farnsworth builds the world's first successful all-electronic television system.
SEPTEMBER: Baird begins experimental broadcasts from his Long Acre studio.
NOVEMBER: Zworykin builds an advanced electronic picture tube, the Kinescope.

## 1930

JULY: Baird demonstrates a low definition large-screen television system.

## 1931

JUNE: Baird televises the Derby.
NOVEMBER: Baird marries Margaret Albu.
Zworykin develops an advanced type of electronic camera, the Iconoscope.

## 1932

MAY: The BBC opens its own TV station to trial a different system from Baird's.
SEPTEMBER: Baird's daughter, Diana, born.

## 1935

MARCH: Germany begins first high-definition TV service in the world.
JULY: Baird's son, Malcolm, born.

## 1936

NOVEMBER: BBC begins regular broadcasts.

## 1937

FEBRUARY: Television Advisory Committee rejects Baird's television system for public broadcasts in favour of Marconi-EMI system.

## 1939

SEPTEMBER: Second World War begins. Television services stop for the duration of the war.

## 1944

Baird demonstrates an electronic television picture tube, the Telechrome, which shows pictures in a limited range of colours.

## 1945

MAY: Second World War ends

## 1946

1 JUNE: Television services resumed.
8 JUNE: Baird televises victory parade.
14 JUNE: Baird dies in Bexhill, England.

## 1949

RCA develops a fully electronic colour receiver.

## 1951

In the United States, the first colour television service is launched, using a mechanical camera.

## 1953

RCA develops an all-electronic colour television camera.

## 1962

The first commercial communications satellite, Telstar, is launched, and relays television signals across the Atlantic.

# Glossary

**Aerial** metal rod or wire that sends or receives radio signals.

**Amplify** to increase in power.

**AT&T** Atlantic Telephone and Telegraph Company.

**Bachelor of Science** someone who has completed a University science course.

**Broadcast** to transmit a radio or TV signal.

**Broadcasting licence** document issued by a government body that permits the holder to broadcast radio or television signals.

**Bronchitis** infection of the lungs.

**Carbon** chemical element that exists in various forms, including diamond.

**Converted** changed.

**Definition** measure of the clarity and sharpness of an image.

**Digital technology** a system in which information is represented by electrical pulses that represent numbers.

**Dynamo** see Generator

**Dysentery** serious infection of the intestines.

**Electrical engineer** an expert in electrical technology.

**Electrocute** to kill by electric shock.

**Electron** tiny electrically-charged particle.

**Electronic television** television system that uses streams of electrons controlled by electromagnetic fields.

**Element** a substance containing atoms that are all of the same type.

**Frequency** basic property of a radio wave.

**Generator** a machine that converts motion into electrical power.

**Homing beacons** Objects that send out signals that planes (for example) can use to find their way to their destinations or targets.

**Infra-red** a type of radiation similar to light, but of longer wavelength. Some infra-red rays can be felt as heat.

**Light detecting cell** a device whose electrical resistance changes depending on the amount of light that falls on it.

**Light ray** a narrow beam of light.

**Light-sensitive cell** an electronic component that reacts to light.

**Mechanical television** television system that uses moving parts (such as spinning discs), together with electrical components.

**Patent** a government agreement that an inventor has the sole rights to make and sell his invention.

**Pneumonia** serious infection of the lungs.

**Presbyterian** branch of the Protestant Church.

**Radio signals** information in the form of radio waves.

**Radio transmission** a radio message that is sent out.

**Radio wave** a wave similar to light, but of much longer wavelength.

**Receiver** an instrument that detects radio signals.

**Resistance** measure of the difficulty with which electricity passes through a substance.

**Royal Institution** a scientific society in the United Kingdom, formed in 1800.

**Scanning** in a television system, the process by which, bit by bit, the brightness (and sometimes the colour) of an object is measured.

**Selenium** metal whose electrical resistance increases when light falls on it.

**Stereo sound** sound reproduced through two loudspeakers, to give a 3D effect.

**Telephone exchange** a place where telephone lines are linked together.

**Televisor** an early name for a television set.

**Temporary** lasting a limited length of time.

**Weather satellite** a satellite used to monitor weather.

# Further Information

**BOOKS FOR YOUNGER READERS**

*Groundbreakers: John Logie Baird*
Struan Reid (Heinemann, 2000)

*John Logie Baird*
Nicola Baxter (Franklin Watts, 2000)

*Super Scientists: Pictures Through the Air*
Anthony Masters (Hodder Wayland, 2001)

**BOOKS FOR OLDER READERS**

*John Logie Baird; Sermons, Soap and Television*
Royal Television Society (latest edition 1988)

*Vision Warrior*
Tom McArthur and Peter Waddell
(Scottish Falcon Books, 1990)

**TO VISIT**

Museum of the Moving Image, London.
This museum is currently closed, but see its
website for news.
**http://www.bfi.org.uk/momi**

The Science Museum
Exhibition Road
London SW7 2DD
Tel: 0870 870468

The National Museum of Photography,
Film and Television
Pictureville
Bradford
West Yorkshire BD1 1NQ
Tel: 01274 202030

**WEBSITES**

**http://www.bbc.co.uk/thenandnow**
A history of the BBC.

**http://www.digitalcentury.com/encyclo/
update/baird.html**
Information about John Logie Baird.

**http://www.dfm.dircon.co.uk**
Early television history, including the earliest TV
recordings, which can be seen playing live on
**http://www.dfm.dircon.co.uk/
recordng.htm**

**http://www.nmsi.ac.uk**
The website of the London Science Museum.

# Index

Numbers in **bold** refer to pictures and captions.